3 4028 08725 2004
HARRIS COUNTY PUBLIC LIBRARY

J 947 Rom
Roman, Carole P.
If you were me and lived
   in... Russia : a child's
   introduction to cultures
                      $9.99
ocn883027905
04/17/2015

If you were me and lived in...

RUSSIA

A Child's Introduction to Cultures Around the World

D1558368

written by **Carole P. Roman**
with assistance from Alexander Luke

Dedication -To Alexander, Hallie, and Cayla- in case you wanted to learn about Laura and Joe.

Special acknowledgment to Alexander Luke and a lovely Saturday spent exploring information about the beautiful land of Russia with his grandmother.

Special Thanks to David at Salon Entourage for all his help. Spasibo! (spa-cee-boo).

Copyright © 2014 Carole P. Roman

All rights reserved.

ISBN: 1493781987

ISBN 13: 9781493781980

If you were me and lived in Russia (rush-a), you would live in Northern Eurasia (Ur-ray-ja). You might call it the Russian Federation because it has many different nationalities and ethnic groups living within its vast borders. Russia is famous for being cold, but it is so big that it has nine different time zones and a variety of climate from warm to cold.

2

You could live in the in the capital city, Moscow (MOS-cow) and people would call you a "muscovite" (mus-co-vite). It is the most populated city in Europe and is the fifth largest city in the world.

If you are a boy, your parents might have chosen to name you Ivan (ee-van), Maxim (max-eem), or Alexander (a-lex-an-der). If your parents needed a girl's name, they could have picked Natalya (Nah-Tal-Ya), Tatiana (tah-chee- ah- nah), or Anya (AAn-yuh).

You would call your mommy, mama (Ma-ma) or mamochka (Ma-moosh-ka), and you would address your daddy, papa (Pa pa) or sometimes papochka (pah-poosh-ka).

If you were me and it was winter, you would want to buy a shapka ushanka (cha-ppa oo-shenk-ka). It is a fur hat with earflaps that tie over the top of your head. It has a thick dense fur that will protect your head if you slip and fall on snow or ice. You would ask mamochka for some rubles (roo-bles) to buy it.

When visitors come to see Moscow, your favorite place to take them would be Red Square.

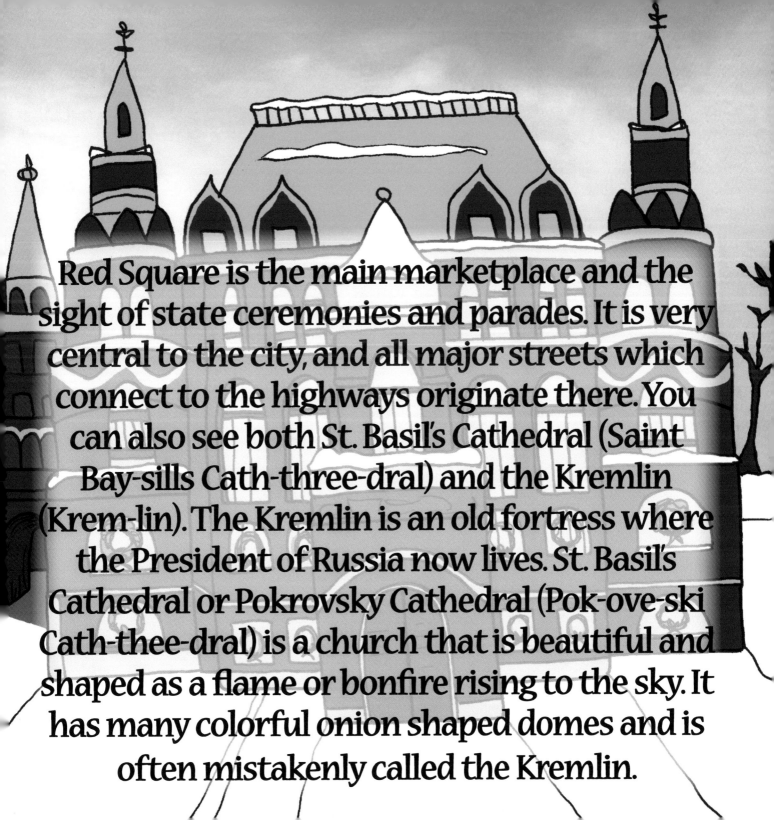

Red Square is the main marketplace and the sight of state ceremonies and parades. It is very central to the city, and all major streets which connect to the highways originate there. You can also see both St. Basil's Cathedral (Saint Bay-sills Cath-three-dral) and the Kremlin (Krem-lin). The Kremlin is an old fortress where the President of Russia now lives. St. Basil's Cathedral or Pokrovsky Cathedral (Pok-ove-ski Cath-thee-dral) is a church that is beautiful and shaped as a flame or bonfire rising to the sky. It has many colorful onion shaped domes and is often mistakenly called the Kremlin.

Afterwards, you would go to eat and probably start your meal with borscht (boor-sc-ht), or beet soup with little bits of meat in it. You would love eating piroshky (peer-rog-ie). They are little pastries filled with potatoes, meat, cabbage, or cheese. Blini (blin-nee), or small pancakes would be on the table and you would roll them with jam, cheese, and if you are lucky, ikra (ee-kra) or caviar (cav-i-ar). Caviar is tiny fish eggs that pop in your mouth when you eat them. You would smother everything with smetana (smet-a-na), which is a rich, sour cream. The meal would finish with tasty tea made from a samovar (sam-o-var) and wonderful syrniki (seer-nik-i). Syrniki is fried dough filled with cottage cheese and dipped in jelly. Yum!

If it's cold, you would call your friends to play hockey on the ice, but you would call it xoken (hook-aye).

16

Chess would also be a popular game, and you would play it often. Your favorite game would have to be fipe (fie- pe). You would count to fifty, while all your friends hide, and then you would look for them. If you touched one of them before they got to the counting place, they would become the new leader. Then the game would start all over and you would hide. Do you have a game like that too?

Your baby sister would love to play with her kuklas (kok-las). She might have a collection of Matryoshka (Mart-tree-osh-kah) dolls. These are hand painted wooden dolls that have little dolls nesting in them.

20

Of course, you would be excited for the many celebrations involving the New Year. It would be a joyous holiday filled with dancing, singing, food and fireworks. You would have a New Year Tree called a Novogodnaya Yolka (nova-god- naya yook-ka) in your home, decorated with treats and topped by a bright star.

You and your family would sing while you wait for Ded Moroz (ded Mor-oz) or Grandfather Frost and his granddaughter Snegurochka (s-neg-ur-coh-ka) to bring presents for under the tree. Maybe your grandmother would cook your favorite meal of meat, green peas, pickles, mixed with mayonnaise, onion, and carrots for dinner. A fortune teller would be invited to tell your future.

You would tell your teacher all about it when you return to shkola (shoo-la).

So you see, if you were me, how life in Russia could really be.

Pronunciation

Alexander-(a-lex-an-der) boy's name in Russia

Anya-(AAn-yuh) girl's name in Russia

Blini-(blin-nee) small pancakes to be eaten with sour cream, eggs caviar and sometimes jelly

borscht-(boor-sc-ht) beetroot soup

Caviar-(cav-i-ar) fish eggs

Ded Moroz-(ded Mor-oz) Grandfather Frost a mythical figure

Eurasia (Ur-ray-ja) Land mass consisting of the continents of Europe and Asia

Fipe-(fie- pe) a game of tag

Ikra-(ee- kra) Russian word for caviar

Ivan-(ee-van) boy's name in Russia

kuklas-(kok-las) doll

Mama-(Ma-ma) mommy

Matryoshka-(Mart-tree-osh-kah) popular hand painted nesting dolls.

Maxim-(max-eem) boy's name in Russia

Momochka-(Ma-moosh-ka) Sweet mommy

Moscow-(MOS-cow) Capital of Russia

Muscovite-(mus-co-vite) person who lives in Moscow

Natalya-(Nah-Tal-Ya) girl's name in Russia

Novogodnaya Yolka-(nova-god- naya yook-ka) New Year Tree decorated with treats and a bright star on top.

Papa-(Pa pa) daddy

Papochka-(pah-poosh-ka) sweet daddy

piroshki-(peer-rog-ie) small pastries filled with meat, cheese, or cabbage.

Pokrovsky Cathedral (Pok-ove-ski Cath-thee-dral) another name for St. Basil's

rubles-(roo-bles) currency in Russia

Russia- (rush-a)- A huge country in Eurasia

Shapka ushanka-(cha-ppa oo-shenk-ka) furred hat with ear flaps that tie over the top of head.

Shkola-(shoo-la) school in Russian

smetana- (smet-a-na) rich, sour cream used as topping.

Snegurochka-(s-neg-ur-coh-ka) His granddaughter

Spacibo- (spa-cee-bo) Thank you

St. Basil's Cathedral (Saint Bay-sills Cath-thee-dral) A beautiful and famous chirch in Moscow. The Russian pronounce it (Sa-bor Va-seelee- ya Bla- zhen-na-va)

Syrniki- (seer-nik-i) fried dough used for dessert with jelly and cheese.

Tatiana-(tah-chee- ah- nah) girl's name in Russia

The Kremlin-(Krem-lin) A fortress in Moscow now used at the home of the President of Russia

Xoken-(hook-aye) hockey

Harris County Public Library
Houston, Texas

CPSIA information can be obtained at www.ICGtesting.com
Printed in the USA
LVIW01n1423270315
432312LV00016B/65

9 781493 781980